PROVEN PLAYER

T0145590

Praises for
PROVEN PLAYER

Living on your own for the first time at college is one of the most confusing times in a young person's life. *Proven Player* is a great way to help navigate that time by keeping you in God's word, helping to remind you that it's His approval we should seek.

—**Casey McGehee**, Major League Baseball Player (Cubs, Brewers, Pirates, Yankees, Miami, and the Detroit Tigers)

Proven Player is a book for leaders. A leader needs to have all the qualities that are presented in this book. This book is a must read for coaches, anyone who is looking for a leader on a team and anyone in a leadership position. I am convinced that to be a great leader you must possess the proven player characteristics.

—**Peggie Gillom-Granderson**, Former Head Women's Basketball Coach at Texas A&M as well as Assistant Coach for the 2000 Women's Olympic Gold Medal Team

Proven Player allows a player who has faith in Jesus to lead their team through times of adversity.

—**Cody Core**, Wide Receiver for Cincinnati Bengals

PROVEN
PLAYER

THE INSTRUCTION MANUAL TO
BUILDING CHARACTER IN SPORTS AND LIFE

JOHN POWELL

NASHVILLE

NEW YORK • MELBOURNE • VANCOUVER

PROVEN PLAYER
THE INSTRUCTION MANUAL TO BUILDING CHARACTER IN SPORTS AND LIFE

© 2018 **JOHN POWELL**

All rights reserved. No portion of this book may be reproduced, stored in a retrieval system, or transmitted in any form or by any means—electronic, mechanical, photocopy, recording, scanning, or other,—except for brief quotations in critical reviews or articles, without the prior written permission of the publisher.

Published in New York, New York, by Morgan James Publishing. Morgan James is a trademark of Morgan James, LLC. www.MorganJamesPublishing.com

The Morgan James Speakers Group can bring authors to your live event. For more information or to book an event visit The Morgan James Speakers Group at www.TheMorganJamesSpeakersGroup.com.

All scripture references were derived from the <u>English Standard Version</u> of the Bible unless otherwise noted.

ISBN 978-1-68350-435-1 paperback
ISBN 978-1-68350-436-8 eBook
Library of Congress Control Number: 2017901533

Cover Design by:
Rachel Lopez
www.r2cdesign.com

Interior Design by:
Bonnie Bushman
The Whole Caboodle Graphic Design

In an effort to support local communities, raise awareness and funds, Morgan James Publishing donates a percentage of all book sales for the life of each book to Habitat for Humanity Peninsula and Greater Williamsburg.

Get involved today! Visit
www.MorganJamesBuilds.com

DEDICATION

Proven Player was an idea which came from my Lord and Savior Jesus Christ. It is to Him that I dedicate this study for the purposes of furthering His Kingdom here on the earth.

TABLE OF CONTENTS

FOREWORD

I first met John Powell when he was the football chaplain at the University of Mississippi. His heart for young men to be fully devoted followers of Jesus Christ was evident in all our conversations. John has invested his life and energies in equipping young men for life on and off the field. This book is a practical resource for personal use, use by a Fellowship of Christian Athletes huddle leader a coach investing in his or her team, athletes from all sports, or a youth pastor seeking to minister to young athletes. Small groups would find these studies a useful tool for discipleship and disciple making

The principles in this book are simple, practical and doable. They are foundational to having a renewed mind and heart. These truths are easily transferable. Once you get them in your spiritual DNA, you can easily impart them to others.

John Powell is helping us live out 2 Timothy 2:2, "The things which you have learned and heard and seen in me, these impart to faithful men who will teach others also."

Michael Catt
Sr. Pastor, Sherwood Church, Albany, Georgia
Executive Producer, Sherwood Pictures

ACKNOWLEDGEMENTS

I would like to acknowledge the following people for their impact on my life, which in turn, impacted the development of *Proven Player*.

Ron Powell, my dad, who from an early age spent countless moments with me on football fields and basketball courts as he taught me the concept of hard work and self discipline.

Tim Enochs and Bruce Tollner for their inclusion of *Proven Player* in their book *On the Clock*.

Hugh Freeze and Ross Bjork along with the coaches, players, and support staff from the 2014 Ole Miss Football season.

My mentor Mike Sparks for his constant life lessons and friendship. Pamela Hall and Lindsay Dawkins who helped as my editor and graphic designer.

Michael Catt for his friendship and willingness to be a part of *Proven Player*.

Morgan and James Publishing Company for allowing the production of *Proven Player*.

Mike Haynes, P.A. Pratt, Larry Shanks, and Vic Wallace who made several deposits in my life as my coaches from junior high through college.

Lastly, my wife Holly along with my children Joanna, Ezra, and Jotham as they walked with me through many long seasons and late nights. Love you!

PROVEN PLAYER
INTRODUCTION

PROVEN PLAYER was first introduced in the book *On the Clock* by Bruce Tollner and Tim Enochs. It was mentioned as one of the resources that had great impact on and brought change to the main character, Adam Alford's, life. Each chapter contains an excerpt from *On the Clock* to show how an athlete's life can be transformed as he or she puts the life principles of *PROVEN PLAYER* into daily practice. *On the Clock* can be purchased at ontheclockbook.com.

THE PROVEN PLAYER

I f most people were honest, we would all acknowledge the inner struggle we have to prove ourselves. We can see this struggle in our ordinary, everyday lifestyles. Whether you are a parent trying to raise your children in a proficient way or a businessperson given a challenging project that others doubt can be done. What about the desire to prove yourself as an athlete to your coaches, teammates, and fans? The list can go on and on. The Proven Player series is designed to help any person overcome the inner struggle to prove oneself. In this devotional, we are going to look at 12 biblical principles derived from the acrostic *PROVEN PLAYER.*

P = Passion – Philippians 3:3-4, 7-9

R = Resilient – 2 Corinthians 12:7-10

O = Opportunistic – Matthew 19:16-30

V = Value – Matthew 13:44-48, Isaiah 49:14-16

E = Eternal Perspective – Psalm 143:3-5

N = Network – 1 Corinthians 15:33, Ecclesiastes 4:12

P = Persistence – Luke 18:1-8

L = Lead – Philippians 3:17, Matthew 23:11

A = Alert – 1 Peter 5:8-9

Y = Yield – Romans 6:13

E = Excellence – Colossians 3:20-24

R = Resolve – Galatians 6:1-10

PASSION

"Peter Alford had a passion for music and Adam Alford had a passion for football. However, the most important passion they had was their love for each other."

Excerpt from *On the Clock*

PASSION

For we…who worship by the Spirit of God and glory in Christ Jesus and put no confidence in the flesh—though I myself have reason for confidence in the flesh also…But whatever gain I had, I counted as loss for the sake of Christ. Indeed, I count everything as loss because of the surpassing worth of knowing Christ Jesus my Lord. For his sake I have suffered the loss of all things and count them as rubbish, in order that I may gain Christ and be found in him, not having a righteousness of my own that comes from the law, but that which comes through faith in Christ, the righteousness from God that depends on faith… Philippians 3:3-4, 7-9

The word *passion* is derived from the word suffer. It can mean a very strong feeling about a person or a thing. I might describe myself as being passionate about football or passionate about my family because I have strong feelings about both. Another term that goes along with passion is the word ambition. Driven by a strong desire to do or to achieve something, ambition requires determination and hard work. We see this passion and ambition in the Apostle Paul in Philippians 3.

Christ has transformed his confidence and created a greater ambition and goal for his life. He states, *"Whatever things were gain to me, those things I have counted as loss for the sake of Christ. More than that, I count all things to be loss in view of the surpassing value of knowing Christ Jesus my Lord, for whom, I have suffered the loss of all things, and count them but rubbish, so that I may gain Christ.*" Paul was passionate about his calling that he was willing to lose everything for Christ Jesus. Like Paul, a Proven Player is someone who is willing to lose everything for his or her passion. Can you say that about your life?

Overtime

Read Philippians 3:3-14

What were the types of things Paul previously based his self-confidence on?

_____

_____

_____

_____

On what type of things are you tempted to build your confidence and identity?

_____

_____

_____

_____

How passionate are you about Jesus? How does this passion define who you are?

_____

_____

_____

_____

RESILIENT

"Resilience is evident during tough times in life. With the help of Jordan Cassidy, his agent, Adam was resilient after learning of his dad's legal issues. As with most things in life, resilience begins with a decision."

Excerpt from *On the Clock*

RESILIENT

Three times I pleaded with the Lord about this, that it should leave me. But he said to me, "My grace is sufficient for you, for my power is made perfect in weakness." Therefore I will boast all the more gladly of my weaknesses, so that the power of Christ may rest upon me. For the sake of Christ, then, I am content with weaknesses, insults, hardships, persecutions, and calamities. For when I am weak, then I am strong. 2 Corinthians 12:8-10

The word *resilient* is the ability to withstand or recover quickly from different conditions. Resilience must be exhibited throughout your life if you are to be a Proven Player. No matter if you are in the heat of battle within your sport or if your children are out of control, you overcome those difficult situations by being resilient. The Apostle Paul understood this and demonstrated resilience in his life. Because of his proclamation of Jesus, he received 39 lashes from a leather strap which included rocks and sharp objects, not only once but five times. He was also beaten with rods and stoned three times, shipwrecked, felt the pressure of caring for the churches he planted, and experienced sleepless nights, hunger, and thirst. In light of what Paul went through, our problems or difficulties may seem insignificant. Yet, we see from his example the ability to withstand struggles and to be resilient.

Life will always throw you trials, painful experiences, and disappointments. While this is true, God has not called us to live in fear or with reservation. Instead, he wants us to be resilient. Paul realized his difficulties paved the way for the Lord to demonstrate his power in and through his life. Therefore, he could say, "I am well content with weaknesses, with insults, with distresses, with persecutions, with difficulties, for Christ's sake; for when I am weak, then I am strong." These powerful words echo within the heart of a Proven Player who is resilient through Jesus Christ.

Overtime

Read 2 Corinthians 11:24-30, 12:7-10

Describe a time when life seemed unbearable and difficult to withstand. How do you try to practice resilience?

_____

_____

_____

_____

After reading about Paul's experiences while sharing the Gospel, how does his example encourage you?

_____

_____

_____

_____

Jesus demonstrates his power in our difficulties and weaknesses. How does this truth empower you to be resilient?

_____

_____

_____

_____

OPPORTUNISTIC

Opportunity knocks. Jordan Cassidy knew he wanted to help young men find purpose in life and follow their dreams. He was in the process of doing what he needed to do to make the move when Adam asked him to be his agent as he makes his move from college football to the NFL. It was time to fast forward the process. Jordan took the leap. Can you hear opportunity knocking? What opportunity is there for you today? What do you need to do?

Excerpt from *On the Clock*

OPPORTUNISTIC

And behold, a man came up to him, saying, "Teacher, what good deed must I do to have eternal life?" And he said to him, "Why do you ask me about what is good? There is only one who is good. If you would enter life, keep the commandments." He said to him, "Which ones?" And Jesus said, "You shall not murder, You shall not commit adultery, You shall not steal, You shall not bear false witness, Honor your father and mother, and, You shall love your neighbor as yourself." The young man said to him, "All these I have kept. What do I still lack?" Jesus said to him, "If you would be perfect, go, sell what you possess and give to the poor, and you will have treasure in heaven; and come, follow me." When the young man heard this he went away sorrowful, for he had great possessions. Matthew 19:16-22

Picture yourself standing close by Jesus when this young man approaches him. He asks a seemingly simple question, *"Teacher, what good deed must I do to have eternal life?"* Jesus tells him to keep the commandments to which the young man responds, *"I have kept them all."* It is at this point when the young man and all those around gasp as Jesus challenges him to give up everything he owns and come follow Him. Can you imagine being asked to give up everything for just one thing?

Like this rich young man, we often focus on what we have to give up to follow Jesus instead of what we get in return.

Focused on his wealth and possessions, the young man could not see Jesus was offering a greater security than worldly wealth. We might even think his mistake was an unwillingness to sell his possessions, but his real mistake was missing out on the opportunity to follow Jesus. That choice caused him to miss an opportunity to receive what he really wanted—eternal life. Jesus was the answer to the question, but the young man failed to evaluate what was being offered.

In sports and in life, we are presented with the option to accept or reject opportunity. Being opportunistic is recognizing and evaluating opportunities and grasping the appropriate ones. A Proven Player, unlike the rich young man, prioritizes opportunities based on the greater implication of following Jesus.

Overtime

Read Matthew 19:16-30

Describe a time in your life where you missed out on an opportunity that you later came to regret.

_____

_____

_____

_____

What were the consequences from that missed opportunity?

_____

_____

_____

_____

What is something that you need to give up because you see an opportunity to follow Jesus?

_____

_____

_____

_____

VALUE

Adam valued family. That was one of the main reasons he wanted to attend Ole Miss and play for Coach Hugh Freeze. He felt a family atmosphere there and wanted to be part of it. Values drive actions. What are your values? What are the core convictions which drive your thoughts and actions?

Excerpt from *On the Clock*

VALUE

"The kingdom of heaven is like treasure hidden in a field, which a man found and covered up. Then in his joy he goes and sells all that he has and buys that field." Matthew 13:44

But Zion said, "The Lord has forsaken me; my Lord has forgotten me." Thus says the Lord, "Can a woman forget her nursing child, that she should have no compassion on the son of her womb? Even these may forget, yet I will not forget you. Behold, I have engraved you on the palms of my hands; your walls are continually before me." Isaiah 49:14-16

Value is considering someone or something to be important or beneficial. In the book of Matthew, Jesus tells a parable about a hidden treasure and a priceless pearl, which are so valuable that two men willingly sell everything they own to purchase them. He conveys the importance of his kingdom and reveals the value of sacrificing for it. Both the man and the merchant were willing to give up everything for something they prized and valued.

Is it possible to know the cost of something, but not know the value? Many believers know the cost for their salvation, but how they live suggests they do not value the kingdom. A Proven Player values and sacrifices for the kingdom of God when he or she understands how much God, our Father, values us. As Isaiah 49:16, reveals we are engraved in the palm of God's hand.

Overtime

Read Matthew 13:44-46

What do you value so much that you are willing to sacrifice for it?

_____

_____

_____

_____

_____

Do you consider yourself valuable to God? Why or why not?

_____

_____

_____

_____

_____

Is there anything in your life that needs to be re-evaluated so that your relationship conveys how much you value Jesus?

_____

_____

_____

_____

_____

ETERNAL PERSPECTIVE

Sometimes tragedy changes our perspective on things. On a stormy day, Adam and Peter's life changed forever. Over time, that change brought about an eternal perspective. What do you think about? Is it just the here and now, or something bigger?

Excerpt from *On the Clock*

ETERNAL PERSPECTIVE

Put not your trust in princes, in a son of man, in whom there is no salvation. When his breath departs, he returns to the earth; on that very day his plans perish. Blessed is he whose help is the God of Jacob, whose hope is in the Lord his God. Psalm 143:3-5

Do you realize that your perspective and the way you view the world affects every aspect of your life? For example, you have a natural tendency to either see life with a positive or negative outlook. Left on your own, your natural tendency will influence and impact how you live and what you do. For this reason, it is crucial to develop and keep an eternal perspective. So what is an eternal perspective? It is looking at every aspect of life from God's point of view. Here's why. Having an eternal perspective will help you know the truth about who you are, the truth about your significance, and the truth about your results.

Who You Are

Placing your endeavors in the hands of men always leaves you vulnerable. An eternal perspective protects you from basing your worth on the temporal or earthly opinions of people. You understand that God's love, forgiveness, and acceptance are the source of your value and worth. Therefore, you are secure. Your worthiness, regardless of performance, is guaranteed because it is rooted in God.

Your Significance

When you look for the world or people to determine your value, your significance defaults to your accomplishments, wealth, career, or social status. With an eternal perspective, your focus is on the person of Jesus Christ and your value is in him; therefore, you can admit your need for help. Your significance is not determined by what you *do*, but what Christ has *done* for you.

Your Results

A temporal perspective leads to constant worry about things like: the score, how you played, and if you were noticed. Success and failure are determined by your results, which are sometimes out of your control. An eternal perspective remembers that the Lord, not your results, defines who you are. It offers a sense of peace to replace worry and frees you to have fun and to enjoy what you do. It also allows you to compete and leave everything on the field because the results do not indicate your worth.

Overtime
Read Psalm 143:3-5

Do you have a temporal or an eternal perspective? How do you know?

_____

_____

_____

_____

_____

What things are you tempted to look for significance in?

_____

_____

_____

_____

_____

How does it feel knowing that Jesus, not your effort, defines your worth?

_____

_____

_____

_____

_____

NETWORK

Jordan Cassidy had a lot of friends because of who he was as a person. His network of friends was one of the major resources he used to help Adam find his way. Who are your friends? Who trusts you? Who can you trust? Who is your network?

Excerpt from *On the Clock*

NETWORK

Do not be misled: "Bad company corrupts good character." 1 Corinthians 15:33 (NIV)

Though one may be overpowered, two can defend themselves. A cord of three strands is not quickly broken. Ecclesiastes 4:12 (NIV)

Network is a group or system of interconnected people or things. The concept of networking is most often associated with advancing up the social or corporate ladder. However, it also happens within a team and a community. A Proven Player recognizes the need for a network of people that can be relied on as he or she navigates the challenges and trials of life.

Experience teaches us that networking can be positive or negative. The Bible affirms this as well. In 1 Corinthians 15:33, the Apostle Paul warned, "*bad company corrupts good character.*" Elsewhere, King Solomon wrote that a cord of three strands is not easily broken (Ecclesiastes 4:12). Solomon, the King of Israel, understood this concept better than most. In ancient cultures, an armor-bearer went into battle with a king. Not only would he carry the king's extra weapons, but also remained by his side during the fight. If an enemy was only wounded, the armor-bearer was responsible for finishing the job. A king would never go into battle alone. He chose an armor-bearer who strengthened him for the fight. In the same way, those who we relate to and spend time with have the potential to strengthen our character. A Proven Player chooses a network of people who add strength to their character rather than weakening it.

Overtime
Read Ecclesiastes 4:9-12

What does your network look like? Who are the people that you have surrounded yourself with? Consider what each one brings to your life and character.

_____

_____

_____

_____

Think about a time when your network of people had a negative or bad effect on you. How did the experience affect your character?

_____

_____

_____

_____

Describe a time when your network helped you. How did this make you stronger and more confident?

_____

_____

_____

_____

PERSISTENCE

Jordan didn't give up on Adam. It's not always easy to stick with something or somebody. Persistence requires something bigger than emotion. It doesn't come from just a feeling but rather a purpose. Jordan had a heartfelt purpose to help Adam and others like him. He didn't give up even when it was hard. Have you even given up on something or somebody? Is there an area in your life where you need to be more persistent? Is it tied to what you believe to be your purpose in life?

Excerpt from *On the Clock*

PERSISTENCE

And he told them a parable to the effect that they ought always to pray and not lose heart. Luke 18:1

Calvin Coolidge stated, "Nothing in this world can take the place of persistence. Talent will not. Nothing is more common than unsuccessful people with talent."

A Proven Player is someone who knows how to persist because they understand what persistence means and what it requires. When a person is persistent, he or she refuses to quit. It is looking into the face of adversity and announcing that you like your odds. Because you believe in your cause, you are unwilling to move aside or give way to distractions.

Jesus taught a parable about persistence in Luke 18. In the story he describes two people, an unruly judge who neither fears God nor respects men and a widow who has been wronged and desires justice. The widow keeps going to the judge pleading her case over and over. Finally exasperated, he gave her an answer because he was tired of her nagging or what Jesus calls persistence. So how does this story relate to you and your life? If you are to be a Proven Player, you must consider how you persist when faced with challenges, adversity or opposition.

In this parable, Jesus was teaching his disciples to pray with the same persistence as the widow had with the judge. We are to go to the Lord with our requests no matter how long or how often it takes. Our prayers may not change our situation immediately, but the time spent with him will change us. Like the widow, we must learn the lesson of not giving up no matter how long it takes.

Overtime

Read Luke 18:1-8

What does your life reveal about your persistence?

_____

_____

_____

_____

Describe a time where you prayed for something expecting a quick answer from God, but had to wait instead. What did you learn about God? What did you learn about yourself?

_____

_____

_____

_____

What needs to take place in your journey to be a more persistent person in your personal life? In your spiritual life?

_____

_____

_____

_____

LEAD

Jordan walked away from a lucrative position with ESPN to give his time helping others achieve and live their dreams. He stepped into a position of leading these young men, beginning with Adam. How does that story resonate in your heart? Is there something you need to do?

Excerpt from *On the Clock*

LEAD

Join together in following my example brothers and just as you have us as a model, keep your eyes on those who live as we do. Philippians 3:17 (NIV)

The greatest among you shall be your servant. Matthew 23:11

Leading is going before or with someone to show them the way. To be a strong leader, you must be able to lead yourself, which includes putting the needs of others before your own. This requires humility, an attribute often divorced from leadership. Yet for those who embrace it, humility not only redefines leadership. It reproduces how they lead. If you want to be a great leader, you must practice humility.

There are many scriptures that affirm humility-based leadership. In Philippians 2:25-30, the Apostle Paul writes about a man named Epaphroditus. Although not much is recorded about him, what is mentioned reveals a man who led with humility. As a leader in the Philippian church, he was tasked with delivering financial support to Paul while he was imprisoned for the gospel. After delivering the gift, Epaphroditus became sick and almost died. According to Paul, only God's mercy saved him and once recovered, God had another mission for him. He was to take back a letter to the Philippians.

In the letter, Paul affirms Epaphroditus describing him as a fellow worker, fellow soldier, the church's messenger and minister. He wrote, *"Receive him then in the Lord with all joy, and hold men like him in high regard because he came close to death for the work of Christ, risking his life to complete what was deficient in your service to me"* (Philippians 2:29). Epaphroditus' humility-based leadership has been useful to both Paul and the Philippians. Choosing to serve others rather than himself, even to the point of death, Epaphroditus demonstrates the qualities of a Proven Player. He models great leadership, one that is to be followed. Notably, he focused on giving rather than getting, putting others needs before his own, and demonstrating how other-centered leadership is a reproducing style of leadership.

Overtime
Read Philippians 3:25-30

If someone were to describe your leadership quality, what terms would they use?

_____

_____

_____

Do you value humility as a quality of leadership? How is this evident in your relationships with those you lead?

_____

_____

_____

Jesus once said, *"Even the Son of Man came not to be served, but to serve and give His life as a ransom"* (Matthew 25:28). If this is true of Jesus, how much more should it be true for us? What do you find most challenging to practicing humility-based leadership?

_____

_____

_____

ALERT

By staying alert adversity did not pull Adam and his dad, Peter, apart, it pulled them together. We all face hard times. Hard times are not fun. But those hard times can make us stronger. What adversity are you currently facing? How can being alert make you stronger?

Excerpt from *On the Clock*

ALERT

Be sober-minded; be watchful. Your adversary the devil prowls around like a roaring lion, seeking someone to devour. Resist him, firm in your faith, knowing that the same kinds of suffering are being experienced by your brotherhood throughout the world. 1 Peter 5:8-9

Most mistakes happen in sports when an individual or team loses focus during game time situations. Someone lets down their guard and becomes inattentive and unaware of what is happening around them. In contrast, a person who is alert notices things others do not, such as potential dangers and difficult situations. They are alert to temptation, lethargy, sluggishness, and apathetic thoughts and behaviors.

Whether in sports or life, a Proven Player is someone who remains alert and focused. As our world changes by becoming increasingly more unsettled, things beyond our control can easily paralyze us. Staying alert helps us confront and manage uncertainty. First Peter 5:8 challenges us to be watchful because we have an enemy, Satan, who is a predator. Just like a lion prowling for prey, the enemy is looking for someone to devour.

Peter reminds us that Satan does not let down his guard. He is alert and watchful just like a lion that waits and watches for potential prey to attack. He waits for the weakest, the slowest, or the most vulnerable. With this metaphor, Peter teaches us to stay alert so we are prepared for the enemy's sudden attack. Once alert, we can resist him by remaining firm in our faith (1 Peter 5:9).

The word firm suggests being immovable, solid, and hard. Through faith we trust Jesus in every situation, whether good or bad. Life's challenges bombard us daily, but a Proven Player is ready. When we are alert and aware of life circumstances, we can be ready to resist the enemy through the power and strength found in Jesus.

Overtime
Read 1 Peter 5:8-9

How aware are you to the circumstances in your life?

_____

_____

_____

_____

_____

Describe a time when failure to remain alert caused difficulty for you. What caused you to let your guard down?

_____

_____

_____

_____

_____

Why is it so important to stay alert when we have an enemy who prowls around and is ready to attack?

_____

_____

_____

_____

_____

YIELD

"Adam yielded to Jordan's wise counsel. Although Jordan didn't tell him what he wanted to hear, he shared wisdom and Adam listened and took action. Where do you need to yield in your life?"

Excerpt from *On the Clock*

YIELD

Do not present your members to sin as instruments for unrighteousness, but present yourselves to God as those who have been brought from death to life, and your members to God as instruments for righteousness. Romans 6:13

YIELD. This is a term that many people shy away from, especially when they consider the true meaning of the word. Yielding encompasses the idea of submission. It can be understood as giving yourself up to something such as a temptation or a habit, but it also means to submit yourself to someone else. In Romans 6:16-18, Paul writes,

Do you not know that when you present yourselves to someone as a servant for obedience, you are a servant to the one whom you obey, either sin resulting in death or of obedience in Christ resulting in righteousness, but thanks be to God that though you were servants of sin, you became obedient from the heart to that form of teaching to which you were committed, and having been freed from sin, you became servants of righteousness.

Paul teaches the Roman Christians that things have changed since they accepted Christ. Before they had no option as to whom they would serve, but in Christ, their sins have been forgiven. Now they can choose through obedience to be enslaved to righteousness. It seems that Paul wants them to ask this question, "Who or what are we yielding to?" If they want to experience life, they must learn to yield or acknowledge the truth of God's word in their hearts and lives.

No matter where we are in life, the question remains the same for us. Who or what are we yielding to? Submitting to God is accepting his truth and obeying it as the way to experience true life. Many things will appeal to our old nature because we still remember what it was like to be enslaved to sin. Yet, God's grace is sufficient and powerful. We have a choice, but we must consider our allegiance. Is it to our old slave master "sin" or is it to Christ, our new master who gives grace upon grace that we may experience eternal life in him?

Overtime

Read Romans 6

Why is the concept of yielding so difficult for a person to accept?

_____

_____

_____

_____

What does it mean to you personally that you have been made righteousness before God through Jesus?

_____

_____

_____

_____

What areas of your life need to change so you can yield to the one true Savior?

_____

_____

_____

_____

EXCELLENCE

Being drafted in the NFL is not just about talent on the field, it's about excellence on and off the field. Talent can only take an athlete so far in sports. Adam was an excellent quarterback, but more was needed. He learned how to focus on excellence on and off the field. In what areas do you focus on excellence? Where do you need to focus more on excellence?

Excerpt from *On the Clock*

EXCELLENCE

Whatever you do, work heartily, as for the Lord and not for men, knowing that from the Lord you will receive the inheritance as your reward. You are serving the Lord Christ. Colossians 3:23-24

Excellence is the quality of being outstanding or extremely good. It is a title of honor. This means excellence is not something you do as much as it is who you are. People are sometimes surprised to find that success does not always mean excellence. The word success is derived from being the best at something and is frequently based on someone else's opinion. Excellence, on the other hand, is defined by *being* your best. We should strive to be better today than we were yesterday. Vince Lombardi said that, "Life's battles don't always go to the stronger or faster man. Sooner or later the man who wins is the one who thinks he can."

The apostle Paul wrote about excellence to the church in Colosse. It seems that some of the believers needed guidance in the work arena. Servants who had become Christians were finding it difficult to work for some of their masters who treated them unfairly. Paul challenged them by teaching, *"Whatever you do, do your work heartily, as for the Lord rather than man"* (Colossians 3:23). Without negating their difficult situation, Paul encouraged the believers to see their effort as being done for the Lord instead of man. Surprisingly, he does not tell them to change the situation, but to remember who they are truly serving.

Excellence does not begin with trying to please man, or ourselves but by remembering we are to work in an excellent way because we serve a sovereign Lord. If excellence is being our best, then we need to stop comparing our situations and ourselves to those who seemingly have it easier or better. Both today and in eternity, Proven Players are those who pursue excellence because God's opinion is truly all that matters.

Overtime

Read Ephesians 6:5-7

How have you mistaken success with excellence? How did this perception influence the way you viewed yourself or others?

_____

_____

_____

_____

Describe a time when you found it difficult to serve someone that was an unpleasant person or boss. In light of what Paul teaches in both Ephesians and Colossians, what difference would it have made to the way you served him or her?

_____

_____

_____

_____

In what areas in your life are you pursuing excellence?

_____

_____

_____

_____

RESOLVE

Adam had to make a decision on his own. He was the only one who could make the decision to do what was necessary to be great on and off the field. For him, for me, and for you, resolve can only happen on the inside. In what areas do you need to come to resolution?

Excerpt from *On the Clock*

RESOLVE

And let us not grow weary of doing good, for in due season we will reap, if we do not give up. Galatians 6:9

A person of resolve is someone who is firm and determined. Life's struggles and difficulties tempt us to give up or throw in the towel, but followers of Christ are to be people of resolve in every situation. We see this in Galatians 6 where the Apostle Paul encourages the Christians to not grow weary. This command precedes bearing one another's burdens, restoring a fallen brother in a spirit of gentleness, and recognizing that we reap what we sow.

Most people do not consider resolve as pertaining to how we treat others. Yet, Paul teaches us that resolve is necessary to not grow weary as we navigate relationships. It is both tiring and wearisome to put others needs before your own. Often, we do not see the benefits of resolve immediately, but we must remember sowing always leads to reaping. Resolve helps us to not grow weary before the harvest comes in according to God's timing not ours. With resolve, we choose to live obediently to God's will in our treatment of others. A Proven Player is someone who is determined and resolved to live today by planting seeds that will grow into a God-honoring harvest in due season.

Overtime
Read Galatians 6:1-10

Think about your relationships. How are you treating the people God has placed in your life? Where do you see resolve helping you or a lack of resolve hurting those relationships?

_____

_____

_____

_____

In thinking about the definition of resolve, how does it relate to not growing weary?

_____

_____

_____

_____

Why is it so important to know that you will reap what you sow? How does this truth encourage you to be resolved in relating to others based on scripture?

_____

_____

_____

_____

ADDENDUM

Additional info for a story?

In 2014, the Ole Miss Rebels battled against Texas A&M in their new stadium with 107,000 screaming fans. The roar and the sheer number of people were overwhelming to the 150 Ole Miss players, coaches, and support staff who saw themselves as out numbered. As the chaplain, I challenged one of our strongest players to break a bundle of Popsicle sticks. When he could not do it, I reminded the team they could overcome the 107,000 by staying united in the battle. Fighting together the Ole Miss Rebels overcame that day and won the battle, 35-20.

PROVEN PLAYER
GAME CHANGER

If we compare our human existence to a game of football, we are all participating in one of four quarters. Some of us are in the first quarter while others may be in overtime. Within every game there is a moment where there is a game changer. In football, it is when a play affects the outcome of the game. In eternal life, it is when a person accepts or receives Jesus Christ as Lord. Please take a few moments to consider where you are in the game. Have you met Jesus, the one who is the ultimate Game Changer? Starting a relationship with Jesus is not about cleaning yourself up or getting your act together. It is about turning to him in faith and believing that what he says is true. Prayerfully consider the following verses and ask Jesus to be your Savior.

1. Accept that you are a sinner.

   "For all have sinned and fallen short of the Glory of God." *Romans 3:23*

2. Believe that God loves you and Jesus died for you.

   "God demonstrated His own love for us in that when we were still sinners Christ died for us." *Romans 5:8*

3. Confess your sin and repent. (turn in the opposite direction)

   "If you confess with your mouth Jesus as Lord and believe that God raised Him from the dead you will be saved." *Romans 10:9*

4. Do away with sinful things in your life which come from this world.

   "Rather, clothe yourselves with the Lord Jesus Christ, and do not think about how to gratify the desires of the flesh." *Romans 13:14*

ABOUT THE AUTHOR

John Powell began playing the game of football when he was nine years old. His passion for the game earned him a football scholarship to Lambuth University where he was an All Conference player and National Collegiate All-Star. He then took a position with the Fellowship of Christian Athletes where he served for over twenty years ending his most recent stint at the University of Mississippi as the football chaplain. At Ole Miss, John led the 2014 football team in a weekly study known as Proven Player. John left Ole miss in the spring of 2015 to join the staff of Fellowship Bible Church as their South Campus Pastor where he resides currently in Jackson Tennessee with his wife Holly, his three children Joanna, Ezra, Jotham, and mother, Beverly.

To find out more about PROVEN PLAYER and other products check us out at provenplayer.com

JOURNAL

Morgan James
Speakers Group

↗ www.TheMorganJamesSpeakersGroup.com

We connect Morgan James published
authors with live and online events
and audiences whom will benefit
from their expertise.

Morgan James makes all of our titles available
through the Library for All Charity Organization.

www.LibraryForAll.org